IT'S TIME TO LEARN ABOUT BLUEBIRDS

It's Time to Learn about Bluebirds

Walter the Educator

Silent King Books
A WhichHead Entertainment Imprint

Copyright © 2025 by Walter the Educator

All rights reserved. No part of this book may be reproduced in any manner whatsoever without written per- mission except in the case of brief quotations embodied in critical articles and reviews.

First Printing, 2024

Disclaimer

This book is a literary work; the story is not about specific persons, locations, situations, and/or circumstances unless mentioned in a historical context. Any resemblance to real persons, locations, situations, and/or circumstances is coincidental. This book is for entertainment and informational purposes only. The author and publisher offer this information without warranties expressed or implied. No matter the grounds, neither the author nor the publisher will be accountable for any losses, injuries, or other damages caused by the reader's use of this book. The use of this book acknowledges an understanding and acceptance of this disclaimer.

It's Time to Learn about Bluebirds is a collectible early learning book by Walter the Educator suitable for all ages belonging to Walter the Educator's Time to Eat Book Series. Collect more books at WaltertheEducator.com

USE THE EXTRA SPACE TO TAKE NOTES AND DOCUMENT YOUR MEMORIES

BLUEBIRDS

High in the trees or near the ground,

It's Time to Learn about
Bluebirds

A little bluebird can be found.

With feathers bright like sky so blue,

It sings a song so sweet and true.

Bluebirds live in woods and fields,

Where open space brings bugs for meals.

They flutter, swoop, and dive with grace,

A happy bird in nature's space.

Their colors shine in morning light,

With soft white bellies, oh so bright!

A reddish chest, a beak so small,

They really are the best of all!

With tiny feet, they perch up high,

Watching insects buzzing by.

They love to snack on bugs and flies,

And berries too, what a surprise!

It's Time to Learn about
Bluebirds

A nest they build inside a tree,

Or in a box so carefully.

With twigs and grass, so soft and round,

A cozy home where eggs are found.

The eggs are blue, just like the sky!

A lovely sight for passersby.

The mother waits, so warm and true,

Until the chicks hatch out brand new!

When babies hatch, they cannot fly,

They stretch their wings and blink their eyes.

Their parents bring them food to eat,

Until they're strong on tiny feet.

Then one bright day, they flap and go,

A brand-new flight, so smooth, not slow!

They soar up high, they sing with cheer,

It's Time to Learn about
Bluebirds

And spread their beauty year by year.

When winter comes, they sometimes leave,

To find a place that will not freeze.

But when it's warm, they come back home,

Where fields and forests let them roam.

So if you see a flash of blue,

Or hear a song that's bright and true,

Just smile and wave and let them be,

It's Time to Learn about
Bluebirds

For bluebirds bring pure joy to thee!

ABOUT THE CREATOR

Walter the Educator is one of the pseudonyms for Walter Anderson. Formally educated in Chemistry, Business, and Education, he is an educator, an author, a diverse entrepreneur, and he is the son of a disabled war veteran. "Walter the Educator" shares his time between educating and creating. He holds interests and owns several creative projects that entertain, enlighten, enhance, and educate, hoping to inspire and motivate you. Follow, find new works, and stay up to date with Walter the Educator™

at WaltertheEducator.com

www.ingramcontent.com/pod-product-compliance
Lightning Source LLC
LaVergne TN
LVHW051919060526
838201LV00060B/4075